The Heart Sutra in Calligraphy

A Visual Appreciation of the Perfection of Wisdom

Nadja Van Ghelue

ECHO POINT BOOKS & MEDIA, LLC

For Núria

Published by Echo Point Books & Media
Brattleboro, Vermont
www.EchoPointBooks.com

Text and calligraphy © 2009, 2018 by Nadja Van Ghelue

The Heart Sutra in Calligraphy
ISBN: 978-1-63561-067-3 (paperback)

Cover design by Adrienne Núñez

Contents

The Heart Sutra 5

The Seal Script 8

Shakyō, the Art of Sutra Copying 11

How to Read the Calligraphy 14

Acknowledgments 14

The Heart Sutra in Calligraphy 15

FULL TEXT: The Great Prajnaparamita Heart Sutra 126

The Heart Sutra

The Heart Sutra is a Buddhist wisdom treasure that we have inherited from the Indian civilization, where a vast literature on Prajnaparamita, the Perfection of Wisdom, was composed between 100 BC and AD 600. This one sutra is the most vivid presentation of the teachings of the historical Buddha—and it is short enough to be contained in one page.

The original text of the Heart Sutra is the Prajnaparamita Hridaya Sutra, written in India around AD 100. Although the author is unknown, the voice of the sutra is the bodhisattva Avalokiteshvara, who is addressing Shariputra, the most learned of all the Buddha's disciples.

Prajnaparamita texts are many. The longest of all, called the Mother, is one hundred thousand lines. The shortest, the One Letter Sutra, condenses the Prajnaparamita teachings into one letter, the seed syllable *A*.* In Sanskrit, *hridaya* is translated as "essence" or "heart," and thus the Prajnaparamita Hridaya Sutra is the Heart of the Perfection of Wisdom teaching.

The Prajnaparamita teaching builds the foundation of Mahayana Buddhism, although historically the Heart Sutra was not always as popular a Mahayana text as it is now. Only in the course of time and through the meditative experience of successive generations of Buddhists did two Prajnaparamita scriptures become increasingly important. One of them is the Diamond Sutra, known in Sanskrit as the Vajracchedika Prajnaparamita, and the second is the Heart Sutra.

Particular to the Prajnaparamita literature is the use of negations, which are not ordinary negations, but instead point to a higher dimension. As in the Heart Sutra, these negations contradict to a large extent our logical reasoning and are meant as a springboard to go beyond linear thought and logic.

The Heart Sutra describes the true nature of reality in the light of the Perfection of Wisdom, which is *emptiness*. To the Western mind, emptiness, or *shunyata* in Sanskrit, is a confusing term in this context, and it has often been misunderstood as nothingness or voidness, although its meaning is just the opposite: wholeness. In the Prajnaparamita teachings the true nature of all phenomena is emptiness; that is, all things are interrelated and depend so completely on all other things that nothing exists by itself as a separate, permanent entity in time and space. Chinese and Japanese have translated *shunyata* using the character *k'ung* and *kū* respectively, which in

---

* A seed syllable is the sound quintessence of a Buddha or deity. It is used to achieve meditative states.

their languages also mean sky or space. Thus, according to the Japanese and Chinese mindset, the character has an expansive, boundless quality.

The direct realization of emptiness is the very base of the bodhisattva path described at the end of the Heart Sutra. The bodhisattva, who strives for enlightenment and has vowed to liberate all sentient beings, relies on nothing but emptiness, the vision of reality attained through the Perfection of Wisdom. At this point, the Heart Sutra gives every seeker of the truth a direct message of spiritual self-empowerment: True liberation starts in our very own mind. Realizing the truth of emptiness from within is the first step toward realizing one's own Buddha nature. Prajnaparamita is thus the Mother of the Buddhas.

Buddha Shakyamuni often compared his teachings to a raft that crosses a river from the shore of ignorance to the shore of enlightenment. In the Heart Sutra, Avalokiteshvara gives us a practical vehicle to help us reach the other side in the form of the wonderful mantra: *Gate Gate, Paragate, Parasangate, Bodhi Svaha.* Although a mantra cannot really be translated because its spiritual power transcends words, the Prajnaparamita mantra literally means, "Gone Gone, Gone Beyond, Gone Completely Beyond, Enlightenment at Last!" With these few words, Avalokiteshvara blessed us with one of the greatest wisdom mantras of the world. The Heart Sutra mantra is the most sacred expression of Prajnaparamita herself, the Goddess of the Perfection of Wisdom. It is a direct key to our Buddha nature, the awakened self. In the sutra it is therefore called the highest mantra, equal to the Awakened One, Buddha, himself.

It is uncertain when the Heart Sutra was introduced to Japan. Beyond a doubt, China acted as an intermediary between India and Japan. The earliest Chinese translation of the Prajnaparamita Hridaya Sutra dates back to the beginnings of the third century of our era. The second translation was made around AD 400 by the monk Kumarajiva, and a third version, based on Kumarajiva's translation, was written by the Chinese monk Hsuan-tsang in AD 649.

Hsuan-tsang is the famous Buddhist monk who in AD 629 set out for India determined to find the true nature of reality. On his long and difficult journey he never separated himself from the Heart Sutra, and whenever he was in danger he recited the sutra or chanted the mantra, upon which it is said the demons, goblins, and bandits he encountered all disappeared. Upon his safe return to China, convinced of the protective power and spiritual depth of the Heart Sutra, Hsuan-tsang produced his own translation. His version became the best-known Chinese translation of the Heart Sutra and was soon introduced to Japan.

Two versions of the Chinese translation have been handed down to us: an earlier, short version, and a later, longer version. The shorter version respects the more revolutionary central character of the original, as it is Avalokiteshvara who teaches, the most venerated bodhisattva of Mahayana Buddhism and the embodiment of compassion. As the Buddhist scholar and translator Red Pine points out, the longer version was written to conform the Heart Sutra to the Buddhist sutra standards. A few extra passages were added at the beginning and end, and it is still Avalokiteshvara who teaches, but this time on behalf of the Buddha, who is present and absorbed in deep meditation. China and Japan use the shorter version of the Heart Sutra. The Japanese version in this book is the original short version, based on the translation of Hsuan-tsang.

Although the Heart Sutra was first translated into Chinese in the third century, the assimilation of the teachings of emptiness into Chinese thought came much later.

The philosophy of *shunyata* (emptiness) was not completely new to the Chinese mind. Many centuries earlier Lao-tzu had already introduced emptiness into Chinese thought; thus Taoist circles could easily adopt the Prajnaparamita teaching. But for the average Chinese, whose mind was deeply rooted in practical and down-to-earth Confucianism, the emptiness teaching was far too metaphysical and too Indian. As D. T. Suzuki says, the *shunyata* system was altogether too high-flown, too vague. To reach the Chinese soul, Chinese Buddhists had to produce their own version of the emptiness teaching. This was the Ch'an school, now known as Zen in the West. The teachings of Zen brought emptiness into ordinary life, into a direct personal experience. Zen masters abandoned philosophical discourses and detailed elaborations on the ultimate truth, and instead pointed to human nature. The famous saying "Directly pointing to the human heart, realizing one's own nature, becoming Buddha," generally attributed to Bodhidharma, expresses this unique message of the emptiness teaching in Zen. With the Sixth Patriarch of Zen in China, Hui-neng, those teachings attained their full character.

When the Heart Sutra and other Mahayana sutras were introduced into Japan in the Nara and Heian periods, Zen had already fully matured in the Chinese mind. Together with other Buddhist schools, it was exported to Japan, where it forged a deep relationship with the Japanese soul.

Today Zen followers study the Heart Sutra, but unlike the early analytical and philosophical school of Indian Buddhism, their approach is simple and direct, through meditative experience.

In one of the Prajnaparamita sutras Buddha Shakyamuni says that upon hearing and understanding the Prajnaparamita teaching one will be overwhelmed with delight, a feeling similar to someone who hears other people recall towns and villages once visited. The delight felt by such a memory points to the fact that in past lives this person was present at the teachings on Prajnaparamita given by the Buddha. My wish is that everyone who reads, hears, and sees the Heart Sutra will feel this joy, as if suddenly remembering something long known but until forgotten.

The Seal Script

When we think of Chinese or Japanese calligraphy, we associate it immediately with rice paper, ink, and brush, although calligraphy, the art of writing, started long before these writing materials were available. To understand seal script as one of the major styles of Chinese and Japanese calligraphy we should take a closer look at the genesis of Chinese characters.

Chinese writing is the oldest writing system on Earth that is still in use today. It has made the leap from engravings on bones in ancient days to encodings on CDs today. Nevertheless, it underwent astonishingly few form changes.

History does not shed much light on the earliest beginnings of Chinese writing. According to a Chinese legend, the characters were originally invented by Ts'ang Chieh, who lived at the time of the mythical Yellow Emperor some five thousand years ago. This legendary sage-inventor of the Chinese characters had four eyes. With one pair of eyes he could observe all the movements of Heaven, the myriad signs of the celestial bodies, and with the other pair he observed all the patterns of Earth, like the tracks of birds in the sand, or the drawings on the shells of tortoises. From this whole vision the first characters for writing were born. Ever since then Chinese have believed their writing to be a manifestation of the divine. To this day, the Chinese and Japanese venerate the written word in a way unknown to the Westerner.

The actual precursor of the seal script is the oracle bone script *chia-ku-wen*, or *kōkotsubun* in Japanese, a shamanistic script found on shells and animal bones. It is the oldest example of the ancient Chinese script and first appeared in the Shang dynasty, around 1400 BC. Small characters were carved into bones, mostly of cattle, or tortoise shells to record the results of divinations.

The *chia-ku-wen* is angular and sharp-edged, due to the hard texture of the bones and shells. The script shows a certain rigidity, but the simplicity and directness of the pictographs grant those oracle bone inscriptions a primal strength. As the first manifestation of calligraphic art in the history of China, they show the natural disposition of the Chinese people toward calligraphic beauty.

Later on in the Chou dynasty (1100–221 BC) characters were engraved in bronze ritual vessels. First the script used was very similar to the *chia-ku-wen*, but a more complex composition of the characters would gradually replace the simplicity of the oracle bone script. The stiffer geometrical structure of the *ku-wen* was loosened up, the lines were arranged and combined in a freer manner, and the characters became rounder. The result was the script called *ta-chuan*, *daiten* in Japanese, or large seal script.

Many bronze vessels with *ta-chuan* inscriptions have been found, particularly in the last century. They prove the existence of several regional variations of this script, which resulted from the calligraphic exploration and achievements of that time. Some of the most remarkable examples of the large seal script on bronze vessels are, for instance, the tripod of the Duke of Mao, known as the Mao-kung Ting, with no less than five hundred characters cast on its interior surface; the Shih-sung Kuei, another bronze sacrificial vase dating from around 800 BC; and the San-shih P'an, a ceremonial vase of the San family of Chou. Needless to say, these bronze inscriptions are invaluable to the calligrapher when studying the large seal script.

Interestingly, during the Chou dynasty, the Chinese had the peculiar habit of engraving the characters on the inside of their sacrificial vessels, mostly at the bottom and very seldom on the outside. It was their delicate way of ensuring that their gods and ancestors could read the message when consuming the offerings of food and wine.

The most remarkable examples of *ta-chuan*, however, are the Stone Drum inscriptions, or *Shih-ku-wen*, engraved on stones shaped like drums. They date back to circa 400 BC and have been praised throughout the history of Chinese art for their exquisite beauty. The Stone Drum characters seem to be alive. They have moved away from static pictographs and become dynamic, organized creatures, harmoniously balancing between concrete and abstract, straight and winding, yin and yang. One can only feel a sense of wonder at such artistic accomplishment, a masterpiece of Chinese calligraphy on stone.

The great seal script was abandoned with the unification of China in 221 BC under the Ch'in empire. The absolutist emperor Ch'in Shih Huang-ti implemented a radical linguistic unification and imposed a new standardized script, called *hsiao-chuan* or small seal, *shōten* in Japanese. This event is significant in the history of Chinese writing as it established for the first time a standard form for each character. From then on, all variations of one single character, commonly used in great seal script, were no longer allowed, and one standard form was made compulsory throughout the whole empire. Compared to the *ta-chuan*, the *hsiao-chuan* is more rectangular, of uniform size, with each character written in an imaginary upright rectangle. The well-balanced patterns are reminiscent of the Stone Drum inscriptions, but their expression is more controlled due to their uniform structure.

Li Ssu, the emperor's prime minister, is believed to be the inventor of *hsiao-chuan*. He is, so to speak, the first known calligrapher, but very few examples of his calligraphy have survived. The most famous is the stone of the mountain T'ai Shan in Shantung of 219 BC, engraved with small seal characters, an exemplary work of the small seal script of the Ch'in.

Meanwhile, silk and small wooden or bamboo tablets had already been introduced as writing materials. One wonders why only very few documents of this kind have survived. Shih Huang-ti, the emperor of the Ch'in, is certainly to be blamed. An adversary of Confucianism, he ordered the burning of most previously published books and destroyed an invaluable calligraphic heritage, allowing the early traces of brush calligraphy to end in smoke.

The efforts of the emperor to establish the *hsiao-chuan* as the only official script did not last long. The increasing administrative tasks of the empire's bureaucratic system called for a faster and easier script, free from aesthetic considerations. The small seal was simply too time consuming. It gradually fell into disuse in the Han dynasty (206 BC–AD 220) and was finally replaced by *li-shu, reisho* in Japanese, or clerical script—a flatter, simplified script. The seal script was restricted to religious or ceremonial occasions and seal carving.

Moreover, the invention of paper in AD 105 changed the very essence of calligraphy. Paper, together with ink and brush, allowed quicker writing, and the new writing styles became more abbreviated. As a result, the seal script in everyday life faded into obscurity.

Nevertheless, its fate changed in the late eighteenth and early nineteenth centuries. The study of the works of old masters has always played an important role in the training of calligraphers. To master the brush, insight in the brush handling of old masters is indispensable. With this intention, calligraphers turned to the seal script engravings in stone and bronze and started to copy them. The very unique feeling of these characters challenged their eyes and hands. To this day the works of these artists have a remarkable modernity.

Two Chinese calligraphers stand out in the seal script renaissance. The talented calligrapher Teng Shih-ju (1739–1805) is famous for his small seal script. His work displays an unmatched beauty, a tranquil oneness with subtle tensions between space and line. The saying "Teng Shih-ju is to seal script what Mencius is to Confucian philosophy" leaves no doubt about his importance in the revival of the *chuan* script.

The second prominent calligrapher is Wu Ch'ang-shuo (1844–1927), genius of the large seal. Unwavering in his study of the Stone Drum inscriptions, he grasped the powerful original expression of this script with his brush and created one of the most sublime, extremely modern expressions of the *ta-chuan*. A great master of calligraphy, stone carving, and painting, Wu Ch'ang-shuo is admired equally in China and Japan.

These calligraphers made an example of the universal, timeless quality of the seal script. Now it is one of the major styles practiced by Chinese and Japanese calligraphers, along with the clerical script (J. *reisho*); regular script (J. *kaisho*); semi-cursive script, also known as current or running script (J. *gyōsho*); and cursive script (J. *sōsho*).

The beauty of the seal script lies in its simplicity, but because of this very simplicity, it is a fragile beauty. Simple beauty implies naturalness, which is the secret of life and strength within the brush stroke. Like the shaman who carved the first pictograms into bones and shells, the calligrapher moves the brush very slowly in the middle of the stroke, creating a central nerve through which vital energy can flow. This is why some calligraphers train in seal script, to achieve a firm control of this brush handling that later on allows them to create with boundless spontaneity. The brush stroke being simple, there is no place to hide.

Shakyō, the Art of Sutra Copying

In Zen meditation the purpose of focusing one's mind on a *koan** is to enable the mind to go from the superficial level of consciousness to the deeper level of intuitive wisdom. Similarly, in the Zen arts practitioners train and discipline themselves to master a method that harmonizes their being with the true self, a "way" that takes them from the limited to the unlimited. First you concentrate on technique, then you integrate the way into your life, and finally the way transforms your life. That's how I see art, as a way that unlocks the full potential of our being.

In the ancient art tradition of China and Japan, calligraphy and paint-

---

* A Zen *koan* is a question that the Zen master asks the student; the *koan* cannot be solved with logical thinking.

ing were methods for integrating body and mind. They were performed as a way to unite yin and yang—Earth and Heaven—within one's very being. Through this union, artists recovered their original innocence and awakened all their creative potential, which otherwise remained dormant. The Chinese painter Shih-t'ao (1641?–1719?) taught the method of the One Brush Stroke* as the basis for true creation. From the philosophical point of view, the One Brush Stroke is the expression of the primordial, the absolute, called "the One" in Taoism, animated by the universal life breath or *chi*. From the artistic point of view, it represents the infinite variety of strokes and dots that render the ongoing metamorphosis of the universe. As the absolute, the One Brush Stroke has no limitations and is only governed by the artist's receptivity of the universe. In Shih-t'ao's *Philosophy of Painting*, the One engenders the myriad of forms and through the myriad of forms the One is experienced. For Shih-t'ao, the sacred arises not from a god or divinity, but is revealed from within the artist, from oneness.

In the West, although art has never been practiced as a "way" as such, some artists did express this experience. Matisse, for example, said that the origin of true art *is* love—love understood as the highest form of intimacy with one's self, a feeling of no-separation, where subject and object disappear and oneness is experienced.

In one of his letters to Picasso he wrote: "In the end, it's not worth trying to be too clever. You are like me: what we are all looking for in art is to rediscover the atmosphere of our First Communion." Asked once if religious art existed, Matisse answered that all art was religious.

As the word "religion" comes from the Latin *religare*, which means to bind or come together, we could thus state that art is actually a religious performance, born from a sense of reunion. As it binds, it allows us to go beyond the limits of the small self and expand to our big mind, which we could call Love, Original Mind, Buddha Mind, or Emptiness. The way of art embraces this quality.

In my experience as artist-calligrapher, I found that Japanese *shakyō* (*sha*, "to copy"; *kyō*, "sutra"), or sutra copying, was an excellent practice of

---

* Shih-t'ao established the method of the One Brush Stroke as a response to the growing academicism in Chinese painting, where copying of old masters had become more important than the experience of the transcendent act of painting itself. In Shih-t'ao's method, the painter should never start painting until he or she unites with the object to be painted through an intense process of contemplation. To be able to grasp this genuine inspiration the painter needs a flexible or "empty" wrist that fully supports this creative impulse. In this technique the wrist and elbow are held above the painting surface, which allows the creative energy to flow freely from the artist's mind through the body and into the brush.

the way of art. Copying the Heart Sutra has played an especially important role in my life, as its subject is precisely this original emptiness.

The present copy of the Heart Sutra is an example of my own sutra copying in the enigmatic ancient seal script. In the East, characters are by themselves considered to be direct manifestations of the primordial, and characters act as messengers between the finite and infinite. I believe the seal script, because of its outspoken directness, has a seed quality that can link us to the primordial wisdom always present within us. To me, *shakyō* of the Heart Sutra in seal script is thus a twofold celebration of the emptiness teachings.

I consider my own *shakyō* practice similar to creating a garden: I plant the seeds of enlightenment, which flourish with each new copy. Now I will take you to this garden.

First of all I clean my workplace and set up the writing table with the things I need for *shakyō*: rice paper, ink stone, fresh ground ink, and brush. I light incense in front of my small Buddha statue, take refuge in the three jewels, Buddha, Dharma, and Sangha,* and I chant the Heart Sutra.

I sit down in front of my writing table and do a short formal meditation, mainly concentrating on the breath. After a while, when I feel calm, I mentally start drawing the *ensō* or Zen circle, symbol of the ever-present awakened quality of the mind. I remain a few minutes with this vibrant image and from that moment on I find myself within the *shakyō* space, where I let go of all expectations of hope and fear. This unbiased mental attitude is the true expression of my Buddha mind, the One-Mind, which during the *shakyō* session will transform into Buddha's activity.

I adopt the right body posture for calligraphy. I slightly spread out the feet on the ground to root myself in the earth and straighten the back to allow the energy to flow unobstructed. Before me lies the rice paper. Fresh ground ink and brush are ready and waiting. I pick up the brush, and to express my deep connection with it for the coming moments I bring it to my forehead and greet it.

I dip the brush in the ink and start copying the sutra. With a clear image of the character in my mind, I brush the first character, then the next one and so on, until the entire Heart Sutra or the part of the sutra I chose to copy is done. My mind is focused and fully present with each single brush stroke. In silence and with awareness I write down the words of the Buddha, and slowly they appear on the blank sheet in artistically shaped images. When doing *shakyō* in this way, the mind becomes very calm and luminous, as if the one who brushes, the figures that are brushed, and the

---

* Dharma refers to the teachings of the Buddha, and Sangha to the enlightened beings.

act of brushing all become one, and outer and inner have disappeared. In this state of full presence the Buddha's speech becomes Buddha's activity, and you experience a wonderful feeling of openness.

The sacredness of sutra copying lies thus not only in the words you brush, which are unique expressions of the Buddha's mind, but also in the way you practice it. When doing *shakyō* you are totally focused on writing; each and every hair of the brush is filled with your whole being. It is this meditative state of mind that allows form to arise from emptiness and to return to it—this is the essence of genuine *shakyō*.

After I finish the sutra copying, I stay quiet and remain for a while in this blissful state of openness and clarity. Then I slowly step out of the *shakyō* brush-meditation and dedicate my practice, making the strong wish that through the virtue of this sutra copying all sentient beings may awaken to ultimate perfect enlightenment.

How to Read the Calligraphy

Traditionally, Chinese and Japanese wrote vertically and from right to left; thus, their books begin where ours end. For obvious reasons this order is impractical in an English book. However, I saw no significant reason to break entirely with this millenary writing tradition in ancient seal script calligraphy. Therefore, on every page the calligraphy is read from top to bottom and from right to left. The pages facing the calligraphy offer each line of the sutra in English, the line in *kaisho*, or regular script, for comparison of ancient and modern calligraphies, and a transliteration of the original Zen chant of the Heart Sutra.

I hope very much that you enjoy the expressive images of the seal script calligraphy and that this book becomes an inspiration to contemplate and meditate on the Heart Sutra.

Acknowledgments

I am especially grateful to Núria Roig, without whose help and encouragement I wouldn't have been able to write this book; to Bill Alexander for his life-saving editing and continuous support; to Yianming Yang for his generous efforts to bring me the best four treasures from China; and to Peter Goodman and Nina Wegner of Stone Bridge Press for giving me the rare opportunity to publish this book on the ancient ways.

The Heart Sutra in Calligraphy

The Great Prajnaparamita

摩訶般若波羅蜜多

maka hannya haramitta

關

腺

麻

寏

豈

𣶒

訶

多

Heart Sutra

心 經

shin gyō

The Bodhisattva Avalokiteshvara,

観自在菩薩
kan-ji-zai bo-satsu

觀自在菩薩

while dwelling in the deep
practice of Prajnaparamita,

行 深 般 若 波 羅 蜜 多 時
gyō jin han-nya ha-ra-mit-ta ji

looked upon the five skandhas,
and seeing that they were empty

照 見 五 蘊 皆 空

shō-ken go un kai kū

皆工貼

空蠶見

was freed from all suffering.

度 一 切 苦 厄

do is-sai ku-yaku

慶藝苟
草古尼

Shariputra,

舍 利 子
sha-ri-shi

form is not different from
emptiness,

色不異空

shiki fu i kū

emptiness is not different from form;

空不異色

kū fu i shiki

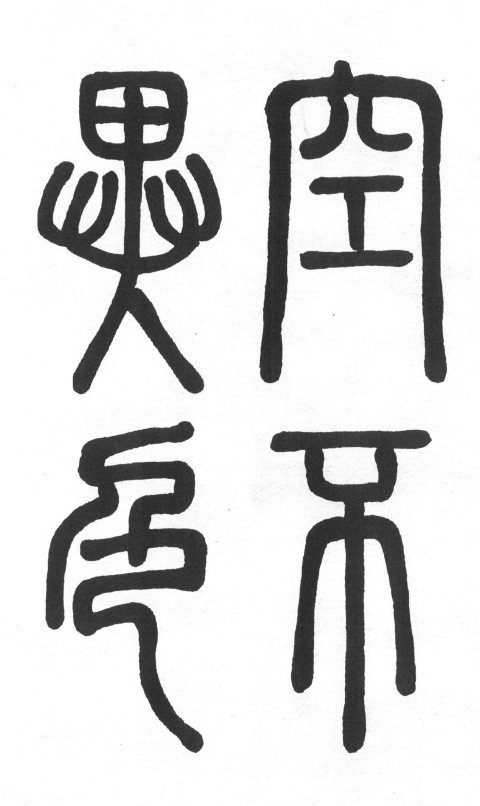

form is emptiness,

色 即 是 空

shiki soku ze kū

是 象

空工 能

emptiness is form.

空 即 是 色

kū soku ze shiki

明朝

The same holds true for
sensation, perception, mental
patterns, and consciousness.

受 想 行 識 亦 復 如 是

ju sō gyō shiki yaku-bu nyo ze

愛　識　如
想　夾　是
你　復

Shariputra,

舍利子
sha-ri-shi

余林子

all dharmas have the nature of
emptiness:

是 諸 法 空 相

ze sho-hō kū-sō

42

是諸法空相

They are not born or destroyed,

不 生 不 滅

fu shō fu metsu

禁禦

not impure or pure,

不垢不淨

fu ku fu jō

秝垢

not complete or incomplete.

不 增 不 減

fu zō fu gen

祁祈

禜壇

Therefore, in emptiness there is
no form,

是 故 空 中 無 色

ze-ko kū chū mu shiki

是故空中無色

no sensation, no perception,
no mental patterns, and no
consciousness;

無 受 想 行 識

mu ju sō gyō shiki

森愛想

林囍

no eye, no ear, no nose, no
tongue, no body, and no mind;

無 眼 耳 鼻 舌 身 意

mu gen ni bi zetsu shin i

朝見鼻祖

甚果苦兒

no form, no sound, no smell, no taste, no feeling, and no thought;

無色聲香味觸法

mu shiki shō kō mi soku hō

蘇　黍　瀟

气　甘　

　味

聲　解

no element of eye,

無眼界

mu gen kai

森眼界

up to no element of
mind-consciousness;

乃至無意識界

nai-shi mu i-shiki kai

乃

坐

森

裏

譏

果

no ignorance,

無 無 明

mu mu-myō

森
森
皿

no end to ignorance,

亦 無 無 明 盡

yaku mu mu-myō jin

大
明

朙

森森

森森

up to no old age and death,

乃至無老死

nai-shi mu rō shi

弘道
考敬

and no end to old age and death;

亦無老死盡

yaku mu rō shi jin

夾森香

胏畫

no suffering, no cause, no
stopping, and no path;

無 苦 集 滅 道

mu ku shū metsu dō

滅 蘇

道 古

藥

no wisdom and no attainment.

無智亦無得

mu chi yaku mu toku

森視

森楢

夾

Therefore, with nothing to be attained,

以 無 所 得 故

i mu-sho toku ko

復故

欲森所

Bodhisattvas

菩提薩埵

bo-dai-sat-ta

薩菩
埵提

rely on Prajnaparamita

依般若波羅蜜多
e han-nya ha-ra-mit-ta

關 朕 修

宮 華

皀 渭

and dwell without mind barriers.

故心無罣礙

ko shin mu kei-gei

燐　棥　故
　　網
　　鄰　也

Without mind barriers

無罣礙故

mu kei-gei ko

隡懋畾故

and thus fearless,

無有恐怖
mu u ku-fu

工巧恐巸

森鬲

翼闈

they see through delusions

遠 離 一 切 顛 倒 夢 想

on-ri is-sai ten-dō mu-sō

遠離顛倒夢想

and finally Nirvana.

究竟涅槃

ku-gyō ne-han

開真從理繁朱

All Buddhas of the past, present,
and future

三 世 諸 佛

san-ze sho butsu

三世諸佛

rely on Prajnaparamita

依般若波羅蜜多
e han-nya ha-ra-mit-ta

險　股　關
　　　寮
　　　巴

and thus awake to unexcelled,

故 得 阿 耨 多 羅

ko toku a-noku-ta-ra

故顓

復宇

阿關

perfect enlightenment.

三藐三菩提
san-myaku san-bo-dai

二

三

Therefore, know Prajnaparamita

故 知 般 若 波 羅 蜜 多
ko chi han-nya ha-ra-mit-ta

關　能　故
寥　此　知
尹　游

as the great sacred mantra,

是 大 神 呪

ze dai jin shu

神是福

祇

the mantra of great knowledge,

是 大 明 呪

ze dai myō shu

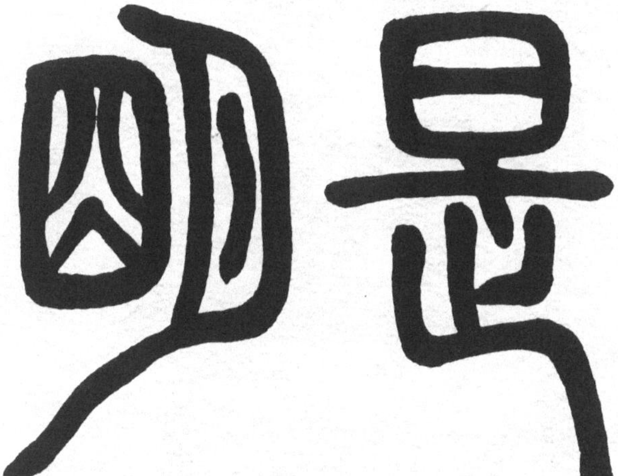

the unexcelled mantra,

是無上呪

ze mu-jō shu

上是門麻

the mantra equal to the
unequaled

是 無 等 等 呪

ze mu-tō-dō shu

是朋友等等森

that frees from all suffering,

能 除 一 切 苦

nō jo is-sai ku

苦蕈切瘶除

true and not false.

真實不虛

shin-jitsu fu ko

眞實不虛

The mantra revealed by
Prajnaparamita

故説般若波羅蜜多呪

ko setsu han-nya ha-ra-mit-ta shu

is spoken thus:

即 説 呪 曰

soku setsu shu watsu

說文解字

"Gate gate,

揭帝揭帝
gya-tei gya-tei

酒誦　酒誦

paragate,

波羅掲帝

ha-ra-gya-tei

游惕誦關

parasangate,

波 羅 僧 揭 帝
ha-ra-sō-gya-tei

游蝙
關蝠
隘誅

bodhi svaha."

菩 提 薩 婆 訶
bo-ji so-wa-ka

菩提薩婆訶　般若

Prajna Heart Sutra.

般 若 心 經

han-nya shin gyō

膀胱經也
經絡也

The Great Prajnaparamita Heart Sutra

Here the separate lines of the English translation that accompany the calligraphy on the preceding pages are presented together.

The Bodhisattva Avalokiteshvara,
while dwelling in the deep practice of Prajnaparamita,
looked upon the five skandhas, and seeing that they were empty
was freed from all suffering.

Shariputra,
form is not different from emptiness,
emptiness is not different from form;
form is emptiness,
emptiness is form.
The same holds true for sensation, perception, mental patterns, and
consciousness.
Shariputra,
all dharmas have the nature of emptiness:
They are not born or destroyed,
not impure or pure,
not complete or incomplete.

Therefore, in emptiness there is no form,
no sensation, no perception, no mental patterns, and no consciousness;
no eye, no ear, no nose, no tongue, no body, and no mind;
no form, no sound, no smell, no taste, no feeling, and no thought;
no element of eye,
up to no element of mind-consciousness;
no ignorance,
no end to ignorance,
up to no old age and death,
and no end to old age and death;
no suffering, no cause, no stopping, and no path;
no wisdom and no attainment.

Therefore, with nothing to be attained,
Bodhisattvas
rely on Prajnaparamita
and dwell without mind barriers.
Without mind barriers
and thus fearless,
they see through delusions
and finally Nirvana.
All Buddhas of the past, present, and future
rely on Prajnaparamita
and thus awake to unexcelled,
perfect enlightenment.

Therefore, know Prajnaparamita
as the great sacred mantra,
the mantra of great knowledge,
the unexcelled mantra,
the mantra equal to the unequaled
that frees from all suffering,
true and not false.
The mantra revealed by Prajnaparamita
is spoken thus:
"Gate gate,
paragate,
parasangate,
bodhi svaha."

Prajna Heart Sutra.

CPSIA information can be obtained
at www.ICGtesting.com
Printed in the USA
LVHW071737241120
672480LV00016B/272

* 9 7 8 1 6 3 5 6 1 0 6 7 3 *